A Lifetime of Words

INSPIRATION

Robin Gorley

© 2011

Acknowledgement

Thank you to my family, and friends for being my inspiration, and for allowing me to share with you my words.

Dedication

I wish to dedicate this book to my Aunt Pat Simpson. She is the light in so many eyes, and has made huge impacts on our lives; especially mine. It is my prayer that you are healed. Love you.

You're My Inspiration

You inspire me always

To be all that I can

And to take nothing for granted

You are my rock

And salvation

Something I have learned

You inspire me always

Never to forget

Who I really am

And always hope for.

The Heavens

Almighty is my God

My light

Looking toward the heaven's

A glow

Prayer the all important

Day and night

Asking to receive

All the love He bestows

Ignoring

Not an option

Wrong, right

Only He can say

My faith, my heart

True to follow

Reign down upon me

Your wisdom, knowledge

Insight

Never to forget what I

All ready know.

Shine Upon Me

The heavens open

The light shines

It is the angels that

Shine upon me.

Heavens hope

Bless me with your wisdom

Protect my soul

Your light

The only defense

Guide and give direction.

Strengthen me

Enlighten my soul

Your vision

My vision

Help me to embrace

The light that shines upon me.

My Heart

My heart has an uncharted path

It sometimes echoes

Deep inside

A piercing wind...

Sharp.

A soul left to feel

A joy of unheard song

The heart unable to anchor

An uncharted path

With no direction

God knows

He has sat the path

I must wait.

God of All

The sun will shine,

The wind blows

Day and night

Comes and goes

The seed human kind

Only to sow

Always guarding

The harp and strings

All that nature brings

The heavens in one accord

God of all

Being of supremacy

The life that pushes on

Only to find strength

In the heart and soul

For me

You are Lord of all!

Someone Said

Someone once said

That you can live

Life without love

Living without love

Is telling God

You don't trust

Life without love

Is for the dying

Living but not loving

Is not the way to hide.

On Top of the Hill

The mansion sits upon

The hill

No walls, just love

Dreams once gone

Stand tall and proud

Complete and perfect.

Someday will one

Day wake only to find that there is

No more sin

I take the hands of

Those I've loved

Only to laugh, play

And give hugs.

What God Gave Me

God gave me the tears

My mother her smile

Paper to write with

Tears and smiles

My tears flow

Although my words don't glow

A smile to make me laugh

My commas fight me back.

My heart begins to beat

My mind begins to write

I wake from my dreams

To write a thought

Before I knew it

From the depth of my breath

The vowels emerge

From the depth of my mind

Consonants sprang.

Time

Our time is short

It is a time to be strong

In what you believe

Our time is short

Between now and then

Your faith must be stable

Our time is short

Learn to fasten your tongue

For time is not to waste

Our time is short

Time to make things right

No excuses

We are no longer sinners.

Our time is short

Demons will arrive

Stand strong

You must keep the spirit.

Our time is short

You know by now

Keep yourself true

To our Lord and Savior

For he knows

Our time is

Not only short...

But coming soon.

Walk Along the Path

Cheerfully I walk along

The pathway

Faithfully asking, knocking

And seeking

To full fill the longing desire

That stirs deep in my soul

Turning steadily to the word

Gleaning the hidden truths

Receiving without measure

God's promised words

Lovingly, God challenges me within

Seeking his spiritual touch

Helping deal with the ways of the world

Only wanting Gods approval.

Holding On

Dedicated to hold

On to the word of God

Which can empower

.
Our souls

Within the spirit of man

Come forth from

God's word

As you flourish spiritually

Lights casting forth

Touching others throughout

Only with the hope of heaven

Capturing life.

For When You Are Weak

When you are weak

Not sure which direction

You need to go

Then in the name of Jesus

Pray

Satan will hear your prayer

But Jesus will prevail

Under no circumstances

Must you let Satan win

Don't be vulnerable

That is when he strikes

When you are feeling weak

Then by all means Pray.

Life to be Enjoyed

Life is to be enjoyed

Laugh, sing, love

Life is to be enjoyed

Has to be decorated

Bare subsistence is not enough

It is not what we have

But what we enjoy

Is what   constitutes

Our abundance.

Enjoy Today and Everyday

Enjoy today

Each day

One day at a time

For who knows

When it's your time

Look to life

For the enjoyment

Of each day

Slow down

It's not only scenery

You'll miss

You'll miss the sense

Of where you're truly going

And why.

Failure

The most successful

Have used failures

As stepping stones

To better things

Most failures

Can be traced

Back to a lack of

Wise thinking beforehand

Too many failures

Is a lack of persistence

Not a lack of talent

Or ability.

Visualization of failure

If you visualize failure

You create

The conditions

To produce failure

Therefore...

Visualize

Believe, and thank God in advance.

For you are no0t a failure

Until you give up

It is possible to defeat fa9ilure

By taking a closer look

To its causes and correcting them

Not by studying

The conditions of success.

Let Me Hear Your Voice

It has been one of those days Lord

As I go about my daily life

Please let me hear your still, small voice

I know you well,

Because I love you

I want to follow your lead

Guide me, I pray

Calm me, remind me

Don't let me go ahead of you

Lead me

Thank you, Lord, for staying near

Me and guiding me

With your still, calming voice.

I Shall Not Want

I shall not want

What you don't me to have

For you know Lord

What I truly need

The Hope We Have

Blessed is the hope

We have within us

To anchor our soul

Steadfast and sure

I found it in

The promises of

My father's written word

The hope we have

Is within our souls

Brighter than any day

God has given us His spirit

I want the world to hear it

All doubts gone away.

You Are The Hope

Hope that is nearly gone, Lord

Reaching down to the lowest

Completely cast down.

At times feeling everything

Is hopeless

Your word assures

Us that nothing is impossible

When we put our trust

In You

Our life is in your hands

You are the hope of all.

The Father Within Your Eyes

Today as I watched you

I seen my father

Within your eyes

Your sense of humor

Your need to work with

Your hands...to create

It only reminds me

As I see my father

Within your eyes

You are my father

Within your eyes

Would We See Jesus

Risen victorious

In all His glory

We declare His glory

His presence upon us

Face to face

To praise his return

We would see Jesus

Powerful name

It is almighty

It is merciful

A glorious name

The powerful name

Of Jesus

As high as the Heaven's

As deep as the depth of sin

Our hearts rebellion

The powerful name of Jesus.

The Majesty of Your Name

What is man,

That you are mindful

Is it the majesty

Of your name or

Something else?

Your name

Transcends the earth

Fills the heavens

Little children

Praise Him

The majestic one

Breath of God

Together we are believers

Our prayers join as one

We trust in the promise

And we believe

Our tongues burn

Our mouth fills with praise

We'll never be the same

Because we have been given

The Breath Of God.

Send Him on Down

So many times

We've gathered here

In the presence

Of the Lord

Can you hear us sing, Lord?

Many times we

Come to you to ask

You for something,

Anything

But this time Lord we sing your praises.

We give You thanks

We give You glory

You are the King of Kings

Send Him on Down!

Promises One By One

You promised to hold

My hand

To help me stand

When life is at

Its ultimate low

You promised

You'd lead me to

The other side

Your promises light

The way

My feet never to stray

Livin' by Your word

I know I'll over come

As long as I stand

On Your promises

One by one.

God Will Make Away

I know there seems no way

God will make a way

When I cannot see

I know He'll work

His ways...

God will make away

He'll hold me close

To his side

And guide me

By His love and strength

I may not always see

God will make away...

No matter where I'll be

In the wilderness

On the road way

He'll lead me always

God will make a way

If the rivers in the desert fade

I know that Heaven

Will always be

Because God will make a way.

I Will Follow Christ

Before the dawn

After the night

It is your face I see

I give you my life

A sacrifice worthy

Only for you

I will follow Christ.

This Is My Son

Your flesh was torn

By the thorns on your brow

My precious child

You're tortured

And bruised body

I'm unable to save you

Although this is not

Your shame

But that of Satan's

It is a sacrificed choice

He must die for us.

Make A Way

Let his glory

Be revealed

Let us lift our hearts

Let us prepare the way

For our Lord is near

Make a way

Lift our voice

Worship and adore him

Let's shout for joy

His everlasting love

Our Lord of life

Make a way.

Perception

What I perceive to be

Is not what God's perceptions are

So I ask God...as I pray

What is it that you need me to perceive

So that I may convey

God has asked me to do what

My heart tells me to do

To not judge 0or be critical of the ones around me

The ones who are involved in my life

God has asked me to trust and

Believe in him

To put things into his hands

So that he may help or solve.

My perception of God is to

Not just pray to him and ask for things

But to0 be obedient, trustworthy

And to give of myself,

So that others may follow.

So I shall not ask

Anymore what God perceives of me

Or what perceptions he requires

Only to trust, and love

Him because He is God.

Behold

Behold! He is coming with the clouds

And every eye will see Him

Ever those who pierced Him

And all the tribes of the earth

Will mourn over Him. Rev. 1:7

Father

Father, when humans have failed me

I tend to blame you for their choices

Please break down the barriers in my heart

That I might worship your Son this Christmas.

Celebration

Lord, as I celebrate your birth, the

Greatest gift I can lay beside

The manger is an act of my will

That makes me your child.

I've been born again.

A Woman of God

You are a woman of God

You were created by Him

And there is no one quite like you,

It is no wonder that God loves you.

You were blessed by Him

And given a mind and spirit

That He wants you to use to the fullest.

Strengthen

Strengthen my faith so that I can love those who don't

Know you, so that I can reveal the true identity of Your Son.

Fall On Me

Spirit of God

Fall on me

That I might lift

My voice in petition

Gifts

Your talent is God's gift to you

What you do with it is your gift back to God

Footfalls

God chooses

Not to come

Royal drums

And blaring trumpets

It is when man

Is silenced

That God's footfalls.

Father Don't Grow Old

You're not old

You have wrinkles

And a few hairs

You're not old

Even though you got dentures

And maybe a cataract

You're not old

Just because you can be forgetful

And sometimes cranky

You are not old

Fathers don't

Grow old

In the hearts

Of their children

They love.

On Angels Wings

On angel wings

Will you fly

Into the sky

With no tears to shed

On angel wings for you are carried

On angel wings you will fly

Into the sky

Holding you tight

Until you take flight.

Books

A Lifetime of Words

A Lifetime of Words: Spirit for the Soul

A Lifetime of Words: Simple Truths

A Lifetime of Words: Capturing the Moments Through a Child

A Lifetime of Words: I Want to Know What Love Is

EBooks

A Lifetime of Words: Spirit for the Soul

A Lifetime of Words: Simple Truths

A Lifetime of Words: Capturing the Moments Through a Child

A Lifetime of Words: I Want to Know What Love Is

A Lifetime of Words: Inspiration

Official Website:

www.alifetimeofwords.com

www.ingramcontent.com/pod-product-compliance
Lightning Source LLC
La Vergne TN
LVHW091211080426
835509LV00006B/941